Make Your Own

Making Masks

Sally Henry and Trevor Cook

PowerKiDS press.

New York

Published in 2011 by The Rosen Publishing Group, Inc.
29 East 21st Street, New York, NY 10010

Text and design: Sally Henry and Trevor Cook
Editor: Joe Harris
U.S. editor: Kara Murray
Photography: Sally Henry and Trevor Cook

Library of Congress Cataloging-in-Publication Data

Henry, Sally.
 Making masks / by Sally Henry and Trevor Cook.
    p. cm. — (Make your own art)
 Includes index.
 ISBN 978-1-4488-1583-8 (library binding) — ISBN 978-1-4488-1613-2 (pbk.) —
ISBN 978-1-4488-1614-9 (6-pack)
 1. Mask making—Juvenile literature. I. Cook, Trevor, 1948- II. Title.
 TT898.H45 2011
 646.4'78—dc22

2010024763

Printed in the United States

SL001621US

CPSIA Compliance Information: Batch #WA11PK: For Further Information contact Rosen Publishing, New York, New York at 1-800-237-9932

Contents

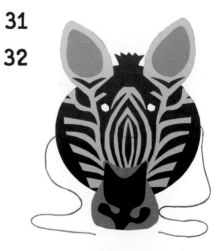

Introduction

Masks are lots of fun to make, and there are lots of opportunities to use them. You can wear them as a costume or make them part of a game.

carnival mask

Paper

Colored paper is a great way to get quick results! Working carefully with scissors and glue can produce a mask in hardly any time at all. See pages 8 and 10.

Many of our masks begin with a kind of **papier-mâché** (say *pay-per-muh-SHAY*), a strong material made with layers of paper and glue. Turn to page 18 to see how we use it to make a mask shape using a balloon as a mold. Then on the following pages we add different features to make a variety of characters.

colored paper

For strong papier-mâché, tear newspaper into strips about 2 by 1 inch (50 x 25 mm). Always tear, rather than cut, your paper for a smooth result. Apply glue evenly but sparingly to the paper. Put down each strip so that it slightly overlaps its neighbor. Make sure that there are no air bubbles trapped between the layers. Five layers should be strong enough for a mask. Allow plenty of time for the glue to dry.

Bulk out details quickly with **tissue paper**. Crumple it up and mix in a little white glue, then cover with paper. Look at how we make Pirate Pete's nose on page 21.

papier-mâché mask

tissue paper

4

Glue sticks

A **glue stick** is a great way to stick paper to paper and paper to card stock. Apply it evenly to one surface and immediately put it in position. Depending on the paper, you may be able to reposition things, but it's always best to get it right first time, if you can!

glue stick

White glue

We've used a glue called **white glue** for our papier-mâché. It's white when it's first applied, but it turns clear as it dries. It makes paper stiff but flexible. If you want your jar of white glue to last longer, you can mix two parts white glue with one part water.

white glue

Card stock and cardboard

Shapes cut from **card stock** or **cardboard** can form the starting point for a mask. Card stock is bendable and like thick paper. Cardboard is thicker, stronger, and stiffer and is often made of layers of card stock. The carnival masks on pages 28–29 started with corrugated cardboard taken from an unwanted box from a package!

cardboard

Soft materials

Felt and **fun foam** (sometimes called EVA) can be bought from craft stores. They come in bright colors and either can be used where soft materials are needed. Cut out details, such as all the features on Fairy Star's face on pages 22–23, and stick them on with white glue.

fun foam and felt

Paint and varnish

Any water-based **paint** can be used for painting your masks. Bright colors often work best when painted on a white background. Cover papier-mâché or cardboard masks made of newspaper with water-based white household paint and allow to dry before applying color. When the paint is dry, make it even brighter by giving your work a coat of **varnish**. Pirate Pete, on pages 20–21, looks better with a matte varnish on his face. The first two black masks on page 28 look great with a glossy varnish. You can use ordinary water-based household varnishes, but paper varnish is ideal. If you want to use glitter, always put it on after the varnish has dried.

water-based paints

Glitter

Glitter can look great when added in the right places. The trick is to make sure the glue is sticky over the whole area you want to add glitter to. It shouldn't be runny or dry. If you're not sure whether you have put enough on, you can add more glue and glitter later!

red glitter

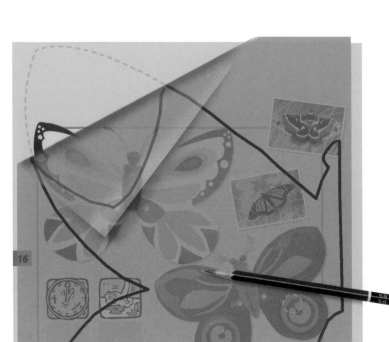

Tracing paper

Some projects in this book come with templates for you to copy. Put a piece of tracing paper over the page and draw along the dotted lines with a soft pencil. Make sure the tracing paper doesn't move while you're doing this. When it's complete, place the tracing paper face down on the surface you want to transfer the drawing to. Draw on the back, following the same lines and pressing firmly. The pressure of the pencil should transfer pencil marks onto the new surface.

6

Tools

We seem to need **scissors** for whatever we're making. Choose a pair with rounded ends. They're safer!

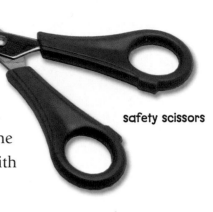

safety scissors

Some things are hard to cut out with scissors and much easier to do with a **craft knife**, such as the eyeholes in the masks on pages 28–29. Always get an adult to help you with knives as they can be dangerous if used incorrectly!

craft knife

A **paper punch** cuts neat holes and makes little round shapes at the same time. Make gold dots by punching gold foil stuck to thin card stock.

gold dots

paper punch

It's a good idea to fix card stock and cardboard together with **staples** as well as glue.

Clean and safe

Find **somewhere to work** that's easy to clean. Glue is hard to clean off fur and fabrics, so avoid carpets, curtains, and pets. A kitchen is an ideal place, but be sure to ask first. Sometimes there's other work being done there! Put sheets of newspaper down to protect work surfaces. Also, before you start, it's a good idea to prepare somewhere to put things while they dry out.

stapler

Easy Mask

30 MINUTES

5 MINUTES

When you put on a mask, you can become someone new and different. How does this new person move? What do they sound like?

You will need:

- Cardboard (cut from a cereal box is fine)
- Pieces of string, about 12 inches (300 mm) long
- Colored paper and card stock • Drinking straws
- Glue stick or white glue • Tape
- Scissors • Markers • Paint and brushes
- Red aerosol cap • Stapler

What to do...

Think of a face you'd like to make. We've decided to make a clown and a cat. We're going to use shapes cut out of colored paper to make our masks very quickly. Wait until all the glue has dried before tying on your mask.

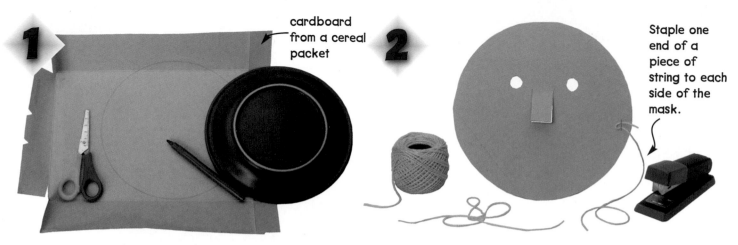

1 cardboard from a cereal packet

2 Staple one end of a piece of string to each side of the mask.

Draw around a plate to make a circle of cardboard about 8 inches (200 mm) across. Cut out the circle.

Cut out eyeholes the same distance apart as your own eyes. Cut a flap for your nose.

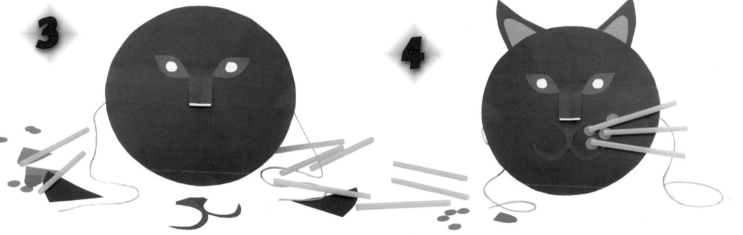

3

4

9

Stick blue paper to the cardboard. Stick pink eyes around the eyeholes. Cut out cardboard ears and stick them on.

Cut out a mouth, tongue, and some little circles from paper and stick them on. Glue on pieces of drinking straw for whiskers.

1 Glue on yellow paper.

Cut the hat from blue cardboard.

2 This aerosol cap is his nose.

The clown is made in the same way as the cat. His hair is made from narrow strips of paper tied together under his hat, which is made of card stock.

Fix the hair and hat in place with a staple. Finally, glue a red aerosol cap onto the nose flap.

Guess the Animal!

Here's a game you can play with your friends. It's a great one for parties!

60 MINUTES

10 MINUTES

You will need:

- Cardboard (cut from a cereal box is fine)
- Pieces of string, about 12 inches (300 mm) long
- Colored paper stock
- Bristles (ours came from an old broom)
- Glue stick or white glue
- Scissors • Stapler
- Markers • Paper punch

What to do...

These masks are made in the same way as the masks on pages 8 and 9. You and your friends can make these and other animals. Then blindfold one friend. Everyone else puts on a mask and acts like that animal. The person in the blindfold guesses who is wearing each mask from the noises each person makes.

Cut the tiger's face and ears from cardboard. Stick orange paper to the face and light brown paper to the ears. Glue down the shapes in this order: white, black, light brown, pink, yellow, and gray. Make the black markings match left to right by cutting shapes out of folded paper.

Here's a zebra. Start by covering the mask with black paper. Glue on cardboard ears, then cut the stripes from white paper. Cut the muzzle shape from more cardboard, and finish by sticking on the nose and mouth, cut from black paper.

Start the owl by covering the mask with brown paper. Cut out the shapes in the picture in black, white, and light brown paper and glue them on. Glue on a pattern of colored paper shapes to make a feather pattern. Don't forget the ears!

The rabbit mask has gray paper glued all over it. Stick on the white and pink paper shapes next. Use bristles from a broom to make whiskers. Make the eyes, nose, and mouth shapes from red and black paper. The white paper teeth go on last!

Butterfly and Moth

Choose the pretty butterfly or the fluffy moth. Use the dotted outlines to make our designs, then you can try copying the real thing!

60 MINUTES

10 MINUTES

You will need:

- *Stiff cardboard, about 17.5 by 10.5 inches (440 x 270 mm)* • *Modeling clay*
- *Colored paper* • *Tracing paper*
- *Paper clip* • *Plastic bottle*
- *Glue stick* • *Scissors*
- *Beads* • *Pencil*

What to do...

The green dotted line on the left is one half of a butterfly, the one in pink on the right is one half of a moth. Choose one of the shapes, trace it onto a piece of paper, and cut it out. This is your template. Check the distance between the eyeholes and make sure you can see clearly.

1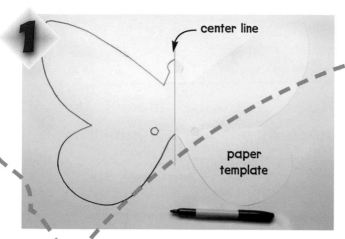

center line

paper template

Lay the straight edge of the template along a center line drawn on the cardboard. Draw around the template then repeat for the other side. Cut around the outline and the eyeholes.

2

Draw loops, curves, and little circles on folded colored paper and cut them out.

3

4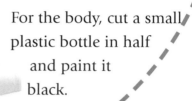

For the body, cut a small plastic bottle in half and paint it black.

Reshape a paper clip, push it through a black bead, and add two blobs of modeling clay to make the head and antennae.

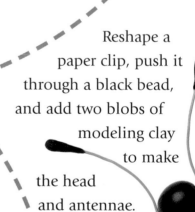

Glue the paper shapes in place with a glue stick.

5

Make a paper loop to fit your head and staple it together. Glue it to the back with the glue stick.

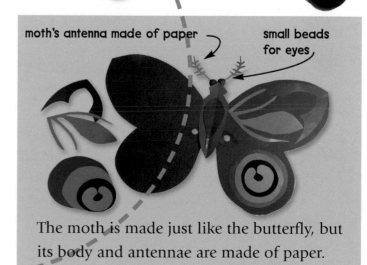

moth's antenna made of paper

small beads for eyes

The moth is made just like the butterfly, but its body and antennae are made of paper.

Robby the Robot

Time to get creative with junk. Let your imagination loose on a robot mask!

60 MINUTES

10 MINUTES

You will need:

- *Shoe box lid*
- *Bits of old toys, models, or computers*
- *Wire, string, elastic • Packaging materials*
- *White glue • Stapler*
- *Objects like corks, bottle tops, or marbles*
- *Aluminum foil • Yogurt containers • Old CDs*

What to do...

Give your mask depth by starting with a shallow box or lid, then glue on all sorts of objects you've found. You need to find things with interesting shapes rather than surface color or pattern because most of it will be covered with shiny foil!

1

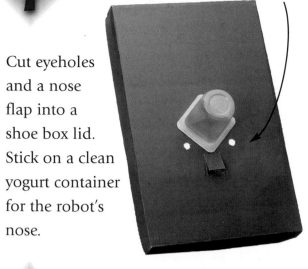

Measure the distance between your eyes. Make the holes that far apart.

Cut eyeholes and a nose flap into a shoe box lid. Stick on a clean yogurt container for the robot's nose.

2

Use white glue to glue on some plastic bottle tops and some chocolate-box packaging.

3

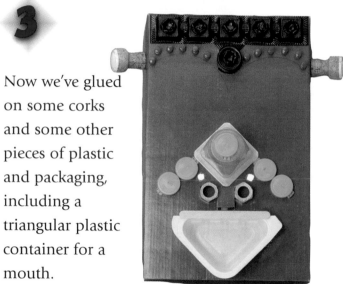

Now we've glued on some corks and some other pieces of plastic and packaging, including a triangular plastic container for a mouth.

4

Cover everything with aluminum foil, pressing it into the shapes. Fold it around the sides and glue down the edges with a glue stick.

5

elastic

15

Now you can get creative with any junk you've been able to find. But make sure nobody needs it first! Use white glue to stick facial features onto the mask. Old CDs make great robot eyes, and we've used spare computer cables and wires for ears and hair (see opposite). Finally, staple a length of elastic to either side of the mask.

Super Specs

Trace this star for steps 5 and 7.

Use old sunglasses to make a great mask. Just make sure you're not using Dad's best pair. They won't be the same when you have finished with them!

60 MINUTES

10 MINUTES

You will need:

- *Old pair of plastic sunglasses*
- *Colored card stock • Glitter*
- *Metal foil paper • White glue • Glue stick*
- *Thin clear plastic • Tape*
- *Scissors • Pencil • Fun foam or felt*

What to do...

Start with a pair of sunglasses that fit you well. They will form the support for the mask so they should also be fairly sturdy. We've found that plastic ones with chunky frames work well. Get an adult to help you pop out the lenses.

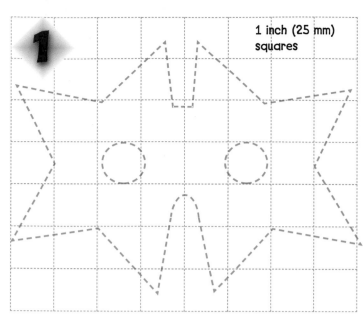

1

Draw a grid in pencil on a piece of card stock. Guided by the grid, draw the mask shape on the card stock.

2

Cut out the shape with scissors.

3

Get an adult to remove the lenses from your sunglasses.

4

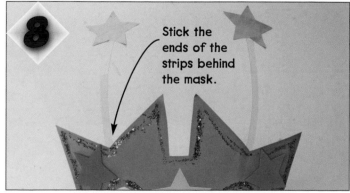

Stick the frame to the card stock shape with white glue.

5

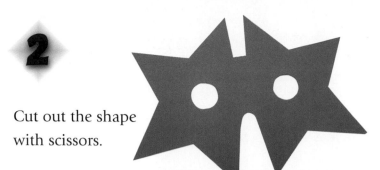

Stick two stars back-to-back on each strip.

Cut two strips of clear plastic. Copy the star on the opposite page onto gold paper. Stick the stars to the ends of the strips.

6

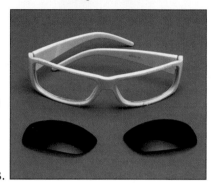

Trace around the edges of the mask with the glue stick, then shake glitter over them.

7

Cut seven more stars out of fun foam. Glue them on the mask with white glue.

8

Stick the ends of the strips behind the mask.

Tape the strips you made in step 5 onto the mask and it's ready to go!

Papier-Mâché Mask

Learn how to make this basic mask, then turn it into any number of different characters.

30 MINUTES

5 MINUTES

You will need:

- Old newspapers • Balloon • Black marker
- White water-based paint and brush
- White glue • Sticky putty
- String or elastic cord • Scissors • Stapler

What to do...

Make several of these masks at once and you can get started on the rest of the projects right away. Take another look at the note about making papier-mâché on page 4 before you start.

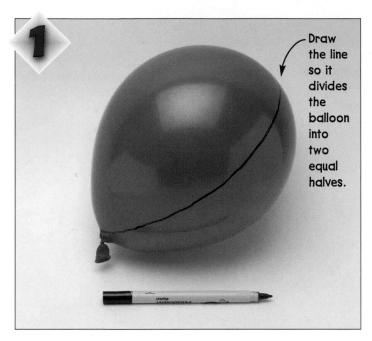

Draw the line so it divides the balloon into two equal halves.

Begin by blowing up a balloon. Draw a line around the balloon with a black marker.

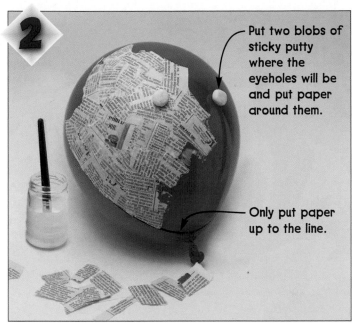

Put two blobs of sticky putty where the eyeholes will be and put paper around them.

Only put paper up to the line.

Tear strips of newspaper .5 by 1 inch (12 x 25 mm) and glue them onto the balloon. Cover half the balloon, slightly overlapping the strips.

Put on five layers of paper and glue. When the mask is completely dry, pop the balloon and pick the putty out of the eyeholes.

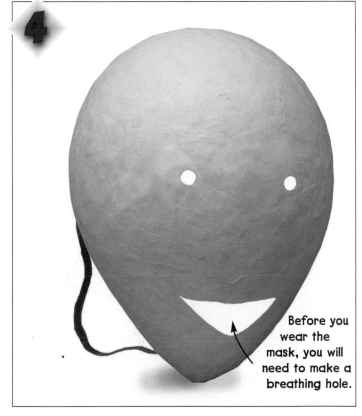

Before you wear the mask, you will need to make a breathing hole.

Neaten up the edges with scissors. Put on a coat of white paint. When it's dry, attach string or elastic with staples. That's one basic mask finished!

Pirate Pete

Pete's a pirate with a hat, an eye patch, a silver earring, and a black beard!

2 HOURS

10 MINUTES

You will need:

- *Plain mask from pages 18–19*
- *Old newspapers • Cardboard • Tissue paper*
- *White glue • Colored felt or fun foam*
- *Paints and brushes • Scissors • Knitting needle*
- *Metal hoop (from a keyring, for example)*
- *Stapler • Black marker • String*

What to do...

Take a plain mask you made in the last project. Make sure it fits well and that you can see through the eyeholes properly. We're going to start by drawing the main features of our pirate's face; his lumpy nose, mouth, two pointy teeth, and mean-looking eyes!

Brush a little glue on a 12 inch-(300 mm) square of tissue paper and crumple it up into a ball. Cover it with newspaper and glue. This is the tip of the nose.

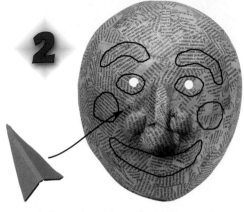

Fold a triangle of cardboard and glue it on the mask above the ball. Shape the nostrils and ears in tissue paper in the same way and cover them with papier-mâché.

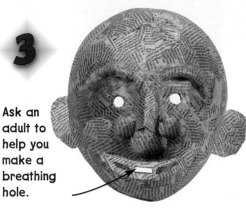

Ask an adult to help you make a breathing hole.

Build up the eyebrows, lips, and teeth with tissue paper. Smooth them over with paper strips and glue. Glue on ear shapes in cardboard and cover them with glue and paper.

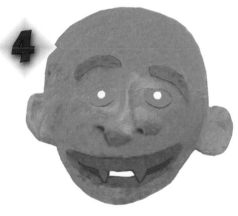

When it's dry, paint the whole mask with a tan flesh color.

Paint the eyes blue, eyebrows brown, and the lips red.

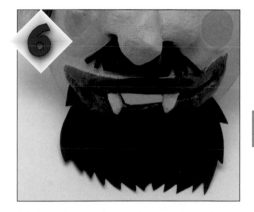

Make the hair and beard with thin fun foam or felt. Glue it in place with white glue.

Take the metal hoop off a keyring. Make a hole in one ear with the knitting needle and hook the metal hoop on. Cut an eye patch from felt or fun foam and thread through some string.

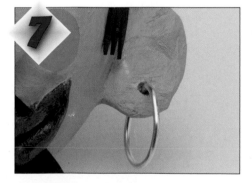

Make a hat shape from felt or fun foam. Cut a skull and cross bones from white felt and glue it to the hat.

staple   staple

Fix the hat on with a staple at each end and some white glue along the bottom edge. Happy pirating!

Fairy Star

How cute can a fairy be?
We need fun foam, a star, and lots of glitter!

45 MINUTES

5 MINUTES

You will need:

- *A plain mask from pages 18–19*
- *Colored fun foam or felt • Colored paper*
- *White glue • Glitter*
- *Thin card stock • Scissors*
- *Fine black marker • Ruler*
- *Paint and brushes*

What to do...

This mask is going to be much more delicate than Pirate Pete and much simpler to make. Cut the shapes directly out of fun foam or felt and glue them on with white glue. It's very quick and easy to get eye-catching results!

1

Paint the basic mask all over in pale pink. Allow it to dry.

2

Draw on the side of the material to be stuck down.

Ask an adult to help you make a breathing hole.

Draw the nose, mouth, and circles for cheeks on colored fun foam or felt. Cut the shapes out and stick them on your mask.

3

Coat eyelids with glue and add glitter before fixing to the mask.

Cut out white and colored eye shapes with holes to match the mask. Make half-circle eyelids and black eyelashes.

4

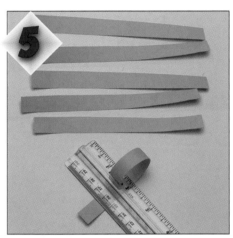

Curve the eyelids as you fix them to the mask. Make eyebrows from fun foam and stick them on.

5

Make hair from yellow paper. Pull strips of paper under a ruler to make them curl.

6

Stick the hair in place.

7

Glue on glitter before gluing the star to the felt.

Make the tiara from colored card stock and a strip of felt.

8

Glue the tiara on. It's finished!

King for a Day

Put on this mask and everyone will have to do as you say!

60 MINUTES

5 MINUTES

You will need:

- *A plain paper mask from pages 18–19*
- *Old newspapers*
- *White glue • Cotton balls*
- *Metallic gold and plain card stock*
- *Fun foam or felt • Black marker pen*
- *Paint and brushes • Scissors • Stapler*

What to do...

Decide what kind of king you want to make. He can be old, young, happy, angry, or silly. You can do whatever you like. You need to start by drawing the features. Don't forget to check for fit and that you can see properly.

1

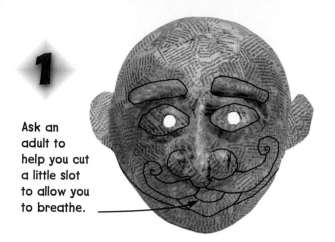

Ask an adult to help you cut a little slot to allow you to breathe.

Draw the eyebrows, nose, mouth, mustache, and beard on the mask and build them using paper and glue, as you did with Pirate Pete. Glue on card stock ear shapes and cover them with paper and glue.

2

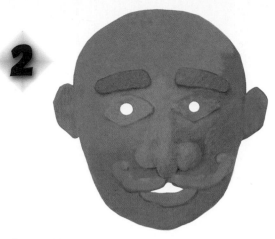

When all the paper is dry, paint the whole mask a dark skin tone.

3

Paint the features very carefully. Keep the eyebrows and mustache the same color.

4

Paint the beard in two shades of brown in wavy lines to look like curly hair.

25

5

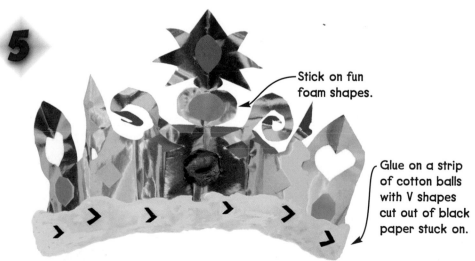

Stick on fun foam shapes.

Glue on a strip of cotton balls with V shapes cut out of black paper stuck on.

Make the crown from gold card stock wide enough to fit the front of the mask. Fasten it with staples. Trim with fun foam and cotton balls.

6

It's finished. Time to start ruling!

Ice Queen

Here's a mask with a very chilly expression!

90 MINUTES

10 MINUTES

You will need:

- A plain paper mask from pages 18–19
- Old newspapers • Scissors
- White glue • Glitter • Card stock
- Aluminum foil • Metallic paper
- Large buttons • Fun foam • Pencil
- Paint and brushes • Black marker • Stapler

What to do...

This time we're going to make a half mask. Your mouth and chin will be showing below the mask.

1

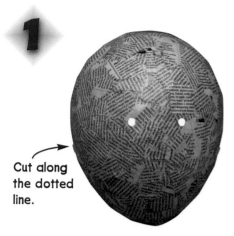

Cut along the dotted line.

Take a plain mask and cut the bottom off with scissors.

2

Build up the facial features with tissue paper and card stock, and cover with newspaper and glue.

3

Color the whole mask a pale bluish green.

4

Make eyelids from fun foam, like the ones used for the Fairy Star, page 23, step 3. Glue the eyelashes to the front edge. Curve the eyelid as you stick it on.

5

Make the hair from aluminum foil strips, about 1 inch (25 mm) wide. Stick one end on the mask, then wind the strip around a pencil to make it curl.

6

Wrap aluminum foil around cones made of paper and stick them behind the card stock crown.

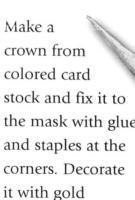

Make a crown from colored card stock and fix it to the mask with glue and staples at the corners. Decorate it with gold ornaments and glitter.

Cover large buttons with metallic paper to make ornaments.

7

It's finished!

Carnival Time!

Carnival is a traditional time in many countries for wearing masks and having lots of fun. This sort of mask can be very simple or very complicated. It's up to you!

30 MINUTES

5 MINUTES

You will need:

- *Cardboard, cardboard tube* • *White glue*
- *Black tissue paper* • *Metallic paper*
- *Sticks about 12 inches (300 mm) long*
- *Straws* • *Elastic cord* • *Scissors* • *Stapler*
- *Plastic jewels, beads, sequins, glitter*
- *Paint, brushes, metallic pen* • *Paper doilies*

What to do...

Copy the green dotted outline onto cardboard and cut it out. This is your template.

1

Cut several mask shapes out of cardboard using the template and glue on a stick or tie an elastic cord onto each one.

2

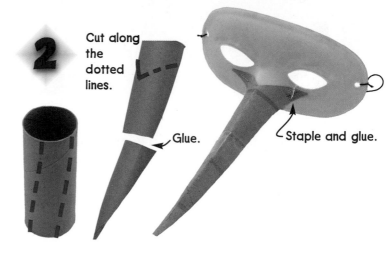

Cut along the dotted lines.

Glue.

Staple and glue.

Cut two long slices off a cardboard tube. Glue them together, then staple the wide end to your mask.

3

Cover the mask with black tissue paper. Using tissue paper keeps the mask light in weight.

4

Decorate your mask with glitter. You can use a pen with metallic ink, too.

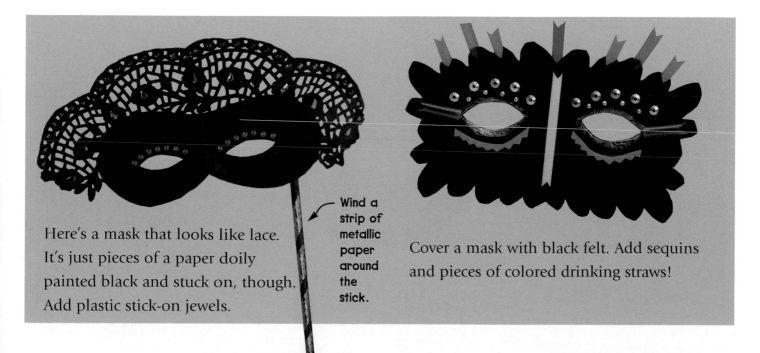

Here's a mask that looks like lace. It's just pieces of a paper doily painted black and stuck on, though. Add plastic stick-on jewels.

Wind a strip of metallic paper around the stick.

Cover a mask with black felt. Add sequins and pieces of colored drinking straws!

Halloween Fright!

These are quick masks to trick or treat in made from paper plates!

You will need:

- *Paper plates – 10 inches (250 mm)*
- *White glue* • *Paper punch*
- *Black marker* • *Paint*
- *Tissue paper* • *Brushes*

What to do...

If you need a mask in a hurry, don't despair! This is a quick and easy way of getting a great mask for Halloween!

10 MINUTES

1 MINUTE

1 Cut out eyeholes. Make a nose flap in the plate and draw the skull design. Punch tie holes.

2 Fill in the design with black paint or marker.

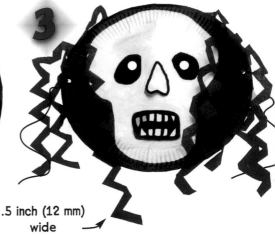

.5 inch (12 mm) wide

3 Stick on purple tissue paper streamers. Tie on strings.

1 Cut holes for the eyes and nose. Draw a pumpkin face on the plate. Punch tie holes.

2 Color the plate orange. Draw the segments.

3 Glue on green tissue paper for leaves. Tie on strings.

Glossary

antennae   (an-TEH-nee) The pair of delicate wandlike structures on an insect's head that it uses for its sense of touch.

carnival   (KAHR-nih-vul) A kind of festival often celebrated with costumes and masks.

corrugated   (KAWR-uh-gayt-ed) Wavy or folded. Flat cardboard becomes much stronger and harder with corrugated paper glued to it.

delicate   (DEH-lih-kit) Easily broken or damaged.

elastic   (ih-LAS-tik) A material that can be stretched easily but will readily return to its former shape, such as rubber.

foil   (FOYL) A very thin sheet of metal.

layers   (LAY-erz) Thicknesses of things.

materials   (muh-TEER-ee-ulz) What things are made of.

mold   (MOHLD) A hollow shape used to help shape something soft or liquid.

papier-mâché   (pay-per-mah-SHAY) A mixture of paper and glue that forms a strong construction material.

robot   (ROH-bot) A machine that can do a complicated task on its own. Some robots are designed to look like human beings, with heads, arms, and legs.

segment   (SEG-ment) One of the parts that go together to make a whole.

staple   (STAY-pul) A kind of wire fastener used for holding sheets of paper or card stock together.

template   (TEM-plut) A version of something that makes it easy to make many copies.

tissue paper   (TIH-shoo PAY-per) A kind of light paper, sometimes used for wrapping delicate objects, but also useful for its decorative qualities.

tracing paper   (TRAYS-ing PAY-per) A special kind of paper that allows you to see an image through it and has a surface that you can draw on in ink or pencil.

varnish   (VAHR-nish) A clear liquid that dries to form a strong protective coating when applied to a surface.

Index

Web Sites

Due to the changing nature of Internet links, PowerKids Press has developed an online list of Web sites related to the subject of this book. This site is updated regularly. Please use this link to access the list:
www.powerkidslinks.com/myoa/masks/